Wheels Around Edinburgh

by
Alan Brotchie

°146

In conjunction with the Corporation tramways, an efficient parcel delivery service was operated throughout the city using smart Morris vans. For a modest fee a parcel could be given to any conductor or handed in to Shrubhill or Annandale Street Central Garage. There was also a network of agents throughout the city and suburbs. This unusual Georgian villa of *c.*1822 stood at 17 Rosefield Avenue, Portobello, just four doors along from the photographer's home. The narrow street prevented him featuring his home, but he was able to set up his tripod in Rosefield Street with sufficient distance to photograph his subject. The house in the picture has been demolished and replaced by a recently constructed villa in a similar style.

ISBN 1 84033 122 4

THE PUBLISHERS REGRET THAT THEY CANNOT SUPPLY
COPIES OF ANY PICTURES FEATURED IN THIS BOOK.

This bus has an interesting story to tell. The vehicle is an 1897/1898 4½ hp Daimler Phoenix which despite being imported from Germany was sold as a 'British Daimler'. It competed with the cable trams on a route from the post office to Haymarket for a 1d fare, with buses on the service known as 'penny stinkers'. The service commenced in May 1898, and was operated by the Edinburgh Autocar Company. They also soon ran to Corstorphine and Newington but got into financial difficulties only to be wound up in December 1903. A re-formed company appears to have operated until at least 1906, and at one stage owned over thirty of these wagonettes. This one was photographed at the east end of Abercrombie Place with its driver Sandy Aitkenhead. The view can be dated to c.1903 as it was in that year that registration numbers were introduced, with 'S' as the Edinburgh identification. 'G' was issued by Glasgow. All Scottish registration-issuing offices were provided with a combination of two letters in a logical alphabetic sequence running from SA for Aberdeenshire to SY for Midlothian then AS for Nairnshire. Towns and cities were added at the end of the list, the final registration being YS for Partick. ('V' used for Lanarkshire is an aberration, and may have been issued prior to the logical series being applied.)

FOREWORD

Wheels Around Edinburgh is an unashamedly personal trip down memory lane where the recurring theme linking each scene is the wheel. The subjects leap from rail, lorry or bus wheel to roller skate or bicycle. Wheels mean movement and transport of both people and merchandise, and the transport revolution allowed workers to live away from their place of work, and materials and goods to be produced further away from their point of consumption. In recent years changes in the transport of goods have allowed, for instance, strawberries to be available all the year round, sometimes by importing them from the opposite side of the earth.

The selection of photographs in this book is largely based upon my own interest in the history of passenger public transport in all its forms, and more particularly with road transport. I have taken the opportunity to illustrate some lesser-known aspects of the transport story, with a reawakening of some childhood memories – including the last red steam lorries hissing and rumbling their way up Elm Row from Leith to Dalry. As a child I also remember some mysterious remnants of the legendary Edinburgh cable tram system, with my questions answered by an indulgent and knowledgeable grandfather. Pictures of cable trams are included.

This selection has been compiled with the aim of drawing together memories, encouraging discussion and perhaps stimulating readers to search attics or store boxes for their own evocative scenes. It is important that memories are recorded – not just photographic images, but also oral recollections. With the twenty-first century heralding increasing change, and virtual reality becoming an ever more common medium, the scenes on the following pages survive as the remaining records of yesterday's everyday. If you come across a photograph which tells a story of Scotland's industrial or transport past, please contact the author via the publisher. Most of these photographs are from my own collection, but thanks must be recorded to R. L. Grieves for assistance and additional material. Several of the photographs were taken by the late E. O. Catford whose glass negatives were given by him to D. L. G. Hunter, and thereafter by Mr Hunter to me. The choice is an entirely personal one, but I hope that it will bring as much pleasure to the reader as it brought satisfaction to me.

This is the earliest image in the selection and dates from the early 1870s. It shows an enormous marine boiler being delivered to Leith, probably to the dry dock off the West Old Dock. The remarkable vertical boiler steam tractor was designed by civil engineer R. W. Thomson and was built locally by Tennant & Co. at their Bowershall works. One of these 6 hp tractors was also used for a short while in 1870 to pull a passenger carrying 'bus', firstly between Edinburgh and Leith, then from Edinburgh to Portobello. The road between Edinburgh and Leith saw the first attempt at local public transport in 1610 when King James granted a patent royal to a Henrie Anderson to run coaches for 2d per passenger between the port and the capital. This apparently didn't last long, and it is a further fifty years before the next reference to such a service appears, at which time William Woodcock was licensed to set up 'Ane haickney coatch for the services of His Majestey's lieges betwixt Leith and Edinburgh'. Public transport on this route is still perhaps the most important in the city.

An animated scene in front of Edinburgh's general post office, with the many spectators focused on the tram turning up North Bridge which appears from its position to have left the rails. Passengers on the upper deck are contributing nothing to assist the conductor who is attempting – on his own apparently, but no doubt with the help of the driver and his horses – to manoeuvre it back to where it should be. The central tram is bound for North Merchiston via Gilmour Place, a service started in August 1882. Note also the 'trace' horse assisting the cart up the 1 in 11 gradient of Leith Street. The foundation stone of the post office building was laid on 23 October 1861 by Albert, Prince Consort and it was at his personal instigation that the massive stone urns were added to embellish the roof balustrade line. The finely-proportioned building opened on 7 May 1866, and acquired an additional storey in 1909.

This picture, probably dating from 1877, shows the original (albeit widened) 1772 North Bridge, photographed from Regent Road at the top of the steps known as Jacob's Ladder. These lead down to the Low Calton and provide a useful shortcut to Waverley. The arches being rebuilt at the south end of the bridge allowed the extension of Jeffrey Street and New Market Street. Demolition of the old Physic Gardens tenements (seen beyond the railway) permitted construction of a much enlarged goods yard. The North Bridge had been widened in 1873, and was further reconstructed in 1894–1896 when the cramped and grossly congested station was completely rebuilt by the North British Railway company. Most of the carriages in the foreground are four wheelers, which were old even when the picture was taken. The 'pots' on their roofs accommodated miserable oil lamps; the North British did not believe in over-cosseting their passengers.

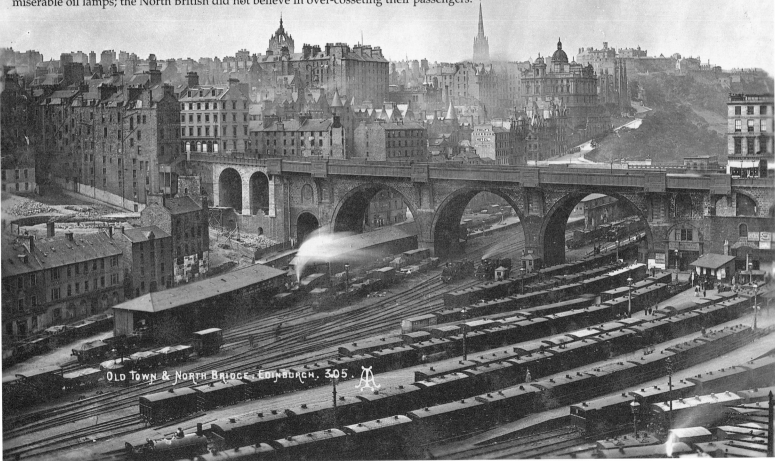

OLD TOWN & NORTH BRIDGE, EDINBURGH. 305.

The west end of the General Station – as the Waverley was originally known – at about the same date as the previous photograph. Before being taken over by the North British Railway in 1865 (which initially used the east end of the station only) the west end was the preserve of the separate Edinburgh and Glasgow Railway Company. A third railway, also originally independent, the Edinburgh, Leith and Newhaven, also gained access to the station by way of the incline tunnel below Scotland Street and St Andrew Street. This company became part of the North British in 1862. The locomotives being used on this (probably Glasgow-bound) train are of the single driver type and could well be two of those obtained following the amalgamation of the NBR and E&GR, possibly built by Beyer Peacock of Manchester c.1860. Waverley Bridge, just visible at the left, is in its original lattice girder state. It was reconstructed into its present plate girder form between 1894 and 1896.

WEST END FROM QUEENSFERRY STREET, EDINBURGH. 117

The West End of Princes Street photographed from Queensferry Street in the last years of the nineteenth century. The only mechanical transport to be seen is the cable tramcar passing in the distance in front of St John's Episcopal Church. The church was constructed in 1818 at a cost of £18,000. This only equates to about £500,000 today; seemingly a remarkable bargain. The sun shades on the left at the corner of Hope Street belonged to Maule & Son, outfitters, and as a trysting place, the invitation to 'Meet me at Maule's corner' later became 'Meet me at Binns'. The four-in-hand horse charabanc on the right in Queensferry Street was most likely on an excursion to view the Forth Bridge. Unfortunately the by-product of horse-drawn traffic is much in evidence in the street, and was something that caused great consternation in all Victorian cities.

Although described as an engineering marvel when it was first constructed, Edinburgh's cable-powered tram system, one of the largest in the world, eventually deteriorated to become a music hall joke. The large number of underground pulleys and mechanical parts ultimately led to problems of wear and tear. Seven long cables under the streets covered the whole 26-mile tram system, and when one broke down every car on that cable stopped. There were cable-driving power stations at Portobello, Tollcross and Shrubhill, whilst the first – dating from 1887 – was in Henderson Row. This picture shows the delivery of a replacement cable there. This worked the cars on the routes from Hanover Street to Goldenacre; Frederick Street to Comely Bank; and Mound to Tollcross. The longest single cable was 34,410 feet long and weighed over 55 tons.

The subterranean cables which kept the cable tramway running required continuous maintenance to ensure minimum disruption. Each curve had a considerable number of directional pulleys. The fastest cable speed was 11¾ mph, whilst the cables driven from Henderson Row ran at only 8 mph. This view of Home Street from Gilmour Place shows work underway at the junction of the Morningside cable (which ran off to the right) with the line to Craiglockhart. The latter line was the last major extension to the cable system, opening in April 1908. Cable car 72, with its covered top, was one of sixteen similar cars built by the tramway company at their Shrubhill works, and is en route from Morningside Station to Abbeyhill in this picture. The scene probably dates from the latter days of the cable system, *c.*1920, with motor transport also in evidence.

Serried rows of Victorian tenements stepping up the hill to Bruntsfield Place (foreground), with Barclay Place and the trees marking the start of Bruntsfield Links on the right. This was another of Edinburgh's many hills which must have caused the horses drawing their loads to ponder the seemingly effortless progress of the stately cable cars. The image is reproduced from a postcard sent on 7 May 1912, and was probably taken not long before that date. The tenements of Barclay Place date from 1890 and were both taller and more ornate than most others of contemporary construction. Certainly they outclass the more typical style opposite. Binnie's coach office stood on the corner, with Miss Butler's 'Servant Registry' next door. Whitehouse Loan had only recently been extended north from Warrender Park Crescent.

The final horse tram route in Edinburgh lasted until August 1907, running from Tollcross to Colinton Road, and becoming the butt of music hall and theatrical humour in the same fashion as later befell the cable tram. This example at the Theatre Royal in Broughton Street shows 'The bus scene' as interpreted by the company of 'Forty Thieves'. One can perhaps forgive them for not quite appreciating the differences between a bus and a tram, and it has to be said that their 'Colinton Road Express' is a fair representation for stage purposes of a contemporary – but even then outmoded – vehicle. The old Theatre Royal was notorious for having been burned out on no less than five occasions – the last on Saturday 30 March 1946, after which it was not rebuilt. Following much public debate as to the use of the site, the John Lewis department store was built in its place.

While Edinburgh persisted with its anachronistic cable trams, the Burgh of Leith decided to go for the latest in urban transport – the electric tram. In 1904 Leith Corporation acquired the horse trams that were currently running in the burgh from the Edinburgh Street Tramways Company, immediately reconstructing them as the most up-to-date models in the area, powered by electricity. From a municipally-owned power station off Junction Street power was supplied to, ultimately, 9.09 miles of route and thirty-seven cars. The first electrified lines were opened officially on 3 November 1905 and by July 1909 the small system was complete. Here two of the new Leith electric trams (numbers 10 and 17) pass in Newhaven Road at the entrance to Victoria Park (left).

A separate electric tramway had been built in 1904, totally supported by private investment. It ran from the cable tram terminus at Joppa, through Musselburgh to Levenhall, and was then extended a further 3 miles to the east end of Port Seton village. The shareholders never got rich from the profits of the enterprise, and whilst the average dividend was a modest 2% there were many years when nothing was paid at all. In contrast to the muted maroon and cream of the cable cars these new trams were painted bright pillar-box red and white, elaborately lined out with gold and white lines. In this sunny view, Musselburgh car 6 – despite indicating that it is going to Portobello – is in fact about to set off for Levenhall. Two ladies stop to pass the time of day beside a small dog cart of the type much used by doctors for house calls. The tram conductor is on the top deck of the electric car, reversing the trolley for the return journey. On the right looms the extravagant architecture of Coillesdene House.

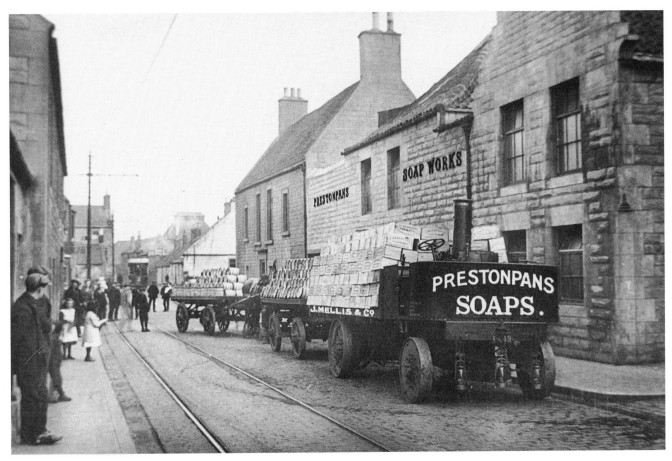

The Musselburgh Electric Tramways were extended in 1909 to run by way of the coastal fishing and mining villages of Prestonpans and Cockenzie to Port Seton, where the company built large tearooms at the terminus to encourage passengers to stay on the car to the end of the line. The narrow streets required the new tramway to be built hard against the footpath, rather than in the more conventional centre of the roadway. Several dwellings had to be demolished to allow construction of the tramway, and one which had a slice removed from its frontage can still be seen. J. Mellis & Co. ran the local soap works and used horse and steam lorries to distribute their product. The steam wagon to the fore is a Sentinel vertical boiler type with a bright brass rim to its chimney. Registered in Lanarkshire (V449) in 1907, steering the solid-tyred vehicle would require a feat of strength from the driver on the uneven roads of that time. Some of these steamers had a boy assistant who acted as stoker, but on most the driver had to do it all. Red-painted Sentinel steam lorries were used by flour millers Herdman on the streets of Edinburgh and Leith until after the Second World War.

Everybody on wheels! Roller-skating on indoor rinks was a pastime invented in the Netherlands, but which became popular in the USA after 1863. There was a craze for it in Britain in the years before the First World War, with several rinks being built or converted from existing buildings in Edinburgh. One (the Royal Park Rink) was located in St Leonard's Lane, whilst this one was in Russell Road. Mr Murray, who sent this postcard to Douglas in the Isle of Man in October 1909, identified himself by a dot on the right-hand side of the scene, just below the Turkish flag. If each skater bought cards then a good number of sales were guaranteed, and getting as many people in the picture as possible was a well-known ploy of postcard publishers of the time.

Being an instructor at a skating rink was a highly sought-after position – think of the glamorous uniform! One of the great attractions of roller-skating was the opportunity it gave to observe and perhaps even talk to members of the opposite gender, and it is no wonder that the older generation looked upon such places as the ultimate in licentiousness. Most socialising at the time took place through the family or the church. Behind the slightly ill-at-ease looking group of six is the exhortation 'If you wish to be graceful, learn to skate', with a board below advising skaters of what they were supposed to be doing – in the main picture the demand is 'All skate'. The precise location of the Russell Road building has not been determined.

Murrayfield Entrance,
Scottish National Exhibition, Edinburgh, 1908.

Over the years Edinburgh staged a number of grand 'International' Exhibitions. At the one on the Meadows in 1886 the latest steam locomotives were dragged through the streets to form exhibits (as was the newest horse tram). The 1890 exhibition was held at Craiglockhart in what became part of the Meggetland playing field. For that occasion one of the Tramway Company's cars was rigged up to work by electricity – a facility that the city had to wait a further thirty years for. In 1908 Saughton Park was the venue for the 'Scottish National Exhibition'. To serve it the Gorgie cable line was extended half a mile to end at the then newly constructed Chesser Avenue. The main entrance to the exhibition was opposite the end of Hutchison Crossway, but there was also an entrance off Balgreen Road south of the railway bridge. The small bus, a 20 hp Halley, ran to and from the car terminus or Haymarket. The Edinburgh Exhibition Motor Service Co., a subsidiary of the Scottish & Irish Motor Service Co., operated the service.

Wheeled transport gets into the picture – just – in this summertime view of Cramond Ferry. A favourite cycle run out from the city, the peaceful, then self-contained, village is still a very popular spot. On the east bank of the River Almond the ferry can be summoned from the far side (where the ferryman lives) and for a modest fee one can be transported across to the Earl of Rosebery's Dalmeny estate for a fine walk along the south shore of the Forth to South Queensferry. Recently at this very spot the present ferryman spotted a piece of carved stone which he initially thought would make a fine garden ornament. On further examination it was found to be a priceless two thousand year old Roman carving of a lion. Now a seminal exhibit in the new Museum of Scotland, it had lain undisturbed for twenty centuries just below this river shingle.

The fish man calls. Peter Victory from Newhaven serving – probably – a maid from one of the large flats in Scotland Street. Much of the street's interest lies in what cannot be seen on the surface. Beneath the centre lies the railway tunnel that was constructed in the early 1840s by the Edinburgh, Leith & Newhaven Railway. Through it a stationary engine drew trains from a station at the foot of the street up the 1:27 gradient to the Canal Street terminus (which eventually became part of Waverley). The tunnel fell into disuse after reorganisation of Waverley in 1868, but the old station at the foot of Scotland Street remained as a coal depot until 1967. Railway posters can be seen on the wall across the foot of the street. The tunnel lay unused for a short time before becoming a successful mushroom farm for many years. During the Second World War it was prepared as a secure bombproof railway control centre, complete with running water and electric power, and more recently a proposal was put forward for it to be used as an underground car park with mechanical car stacking. Peter Victory went on to become a well-known local taxi operator.

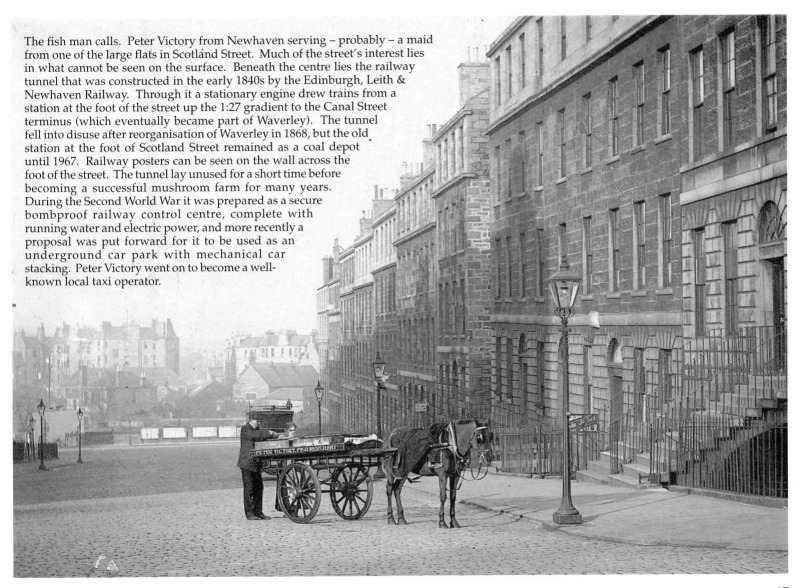

The first charabanc purchased by the Corporation was this 27 seat Leyland (B8725) seen on a 'proving' trip at the then un-built up West Mains Road. It arrived in August 1919 and was immediately used along with two others (S9257–8) on tours of the city. A choice of two tours was offered, either of the southern suburbs, or of those to the north, at a fare of 1s 0d. The vehicles were also in demand to augment the cable trams when these were under pressure from football match traffic.

A mining industry dispute from April to July 1921 made it extremely difficult for the cable power stations which operated the city tramways to get hold of supplies of coal. The action – never considered as a 'strike' by miners, always a lock-out by the employers – caused much bitterness. The 'Triple Alliance' of miners, NUR railway workers and the road transport Workers Federation failed to exert the combined action which had been anticipated by the miners. Troops were seen on the streets in mining areas as the government of the day anticipated anarchy – or even revolution (this was after all only four years after the Russian revolution). The miners even took out in sympathy the enginemen tending the pumps which kept the pits dry – a foolish move which hardened attitudes, caused considerable damage and meant ultimately that jobs were lost. Road transport was not blocked and the Corporation was able to send lorries and converted charabancs to the pitheads to uplift coal. Here B8725 (seen in pristine condition on the opposite page), is pictured at one of the Edinburgh Coal Company's collieries – possibly Carberry.

Thousands of privately-owned coal (and other merchandise) wagons clogged up the country's railway system as they usually had to be worked empty from the coal depot to the mine while the mine owner had hundreds of laden wagons leaving and returning empty. The result of this was that mine-owners could never be guaranteed an adequate supply of wagons when required, so a need was created for dedicated fleets, which for some large companies numbered thousands. Coal was mined to meet the variances of supply and demand and without wagon availability had to be stockpiled near the pit-head, resulting in the extra expense of double handling. Edinburgh's sobriquet of 'Auld Reekie' came about because of its innumerable coal fires. These were fuelled by merchants operating from several rail-served depots throughout the city. One such was St Leonard's, the former terminus of the pioneer (1831) Edinburgh and Dalkeith Railway, which lost its passenger service as early as 1860. As a coal depot, however, St Leonard's served for a further hundred years. Peter McIntosh was one of several merchants based there. Some merchants identified their wagons in gaudy green, blue or red, but McIntosh's were painted with the more conventional brown oxide paint.

The *Scotsman* was first published on 25 January 1817 at the not inconsiderable price of 10d. The prospectus of 30 November the previous year advised that 'the Conductors of THE SCOTSMAN will endeavour "to hold the mirror up to nature," and exhibit as much as possible, "the very shape and pressure of the times." ' A 'Nota' to the prospectus adds – 'after something more than a year's experience, the Projectors . . . feel great pleasure in being able to state that they have not been disappointed in the appeal made to the public spirit of their countrymen in 1816'. Pages were numbered consecutively and an index was provided. At the turn of the twentieth century, publication was moved to purpose-built premises at the south end of the North Bridge. The printing rooms in the four floors below brought the finished newspapers out at Market Street, or below to a specially constructed railway siding off Waverley Station from which special 'Scotsman' trains with their own dedicated vans departed. In November 1919 the proprietors invested in this 20 hp Albion 30 cwt lorry, model type A16. Note the ready-to-hand fire extinguisher. Fire was an ever-present problem with petrol-fuelled vehicles (although the problem of fires lessened with increased use of the diesel engine).

An integrated transport interchange? Not planned as such, this stopgap measure was necessary following reluctance to invest in an extension from the long-established Murrayfield cable tram terminus. Murrayfield terminus, seen here in the summer of 1920, was at the foot of Ellersly Road, which had been the city boundary when the tramway was built twenty years before. Route 1 ran across the city to Nether Liberton on the south side. Note the 'CARS STOP' sign high on the lamp pole – somewhat superfluous here as there was no more track! The two Corporation 31 seat Leyland buses (S9310 and S9320 behind) were running a shuttle service from the tram terminus to the Scottish National Zoological Park. Developed from 1913, the 'zoo' was then, and remains today, a favourite venue for a day out.

Salisbury Place, Edinburgh. M. 514.

For years Salisbury Place off Newington Road was treated as a short working turning point for trams on the busy Newington Station and Liberton route. It also provided a part route terminus for cars on route 5 which would normally continue on to Churchhill or Morningside Station. Note Wood Brothers' delivery van outside their butcher's shop on the corner. Parking here today would probably result in the vehicle being towed to the police pound. Traffic then was controlled by a points policeman who does not appear to be over-taxed. The bakery aromas formerly emanating from the Middlemass biscuit factory have long dissipated, and the building has been replaced by the like-it or loathe-it architecture of the Scottish National Library Map Department building. Opposite, the former Longmore Hospital has been given a new lease of life as the headquarters of Historic Scotland.

Excitement in Gorgie Road at the top of McLeod Street c.1924 with a water mains burst providing entertainment for a large crowd. The impressive Scott motorcycle and sidecar combination recalls the days before wearing safety helmets was made compulsory – when a trilby, or even a back-to-front flat cap, appeared totally acceptable – or even de rigueur. Tram 283 was built in 1923 and had the open ends of its top deck enclosed c.1929. Behind the tram is the bridge carrying the LMS (former Caledonian) railway line from Slateford to Haymarket – not much used then, but now a vital section of the rail network following the closure of Princes Street Station. This required the re-routing of all its traffic, and the transfer of West Coast Main Line services to and from Waverley. Behind the Gorgie Road tenements on the left lies Tynecastle Park – home of Heart of Midlothian Football Club. It may be an apocryphal story that the colour chosen for Edinburgh's transport vehicles (maroon or madder) was taken from the Hearts strip. Can anybody confirm?

The capacity of Edinburgh's tram fleet was phenomenal. For football and rugby matches scores of trams carried the faithful to Tynecastle or Murrayfield (but less so to Easter Road, which was not so closely served by the tram system). Prior to construction of the George Street 'bypass' line in July 1925, specials lined up at Waverley steps; thereafter St Andrew Square became the loading point with an unending stream of cars heading west along George Street. After the match, with the traffic direction reversed, preparations were made by parking trams either at Gorgie (for Tynecastle) or Corstorphine (for Murrayfield) to await the final whistle. The Corstorphine streets were deserted when this photograph was taken on Saturday 3 February 1934; apart that is from the poised armada of trams awaiting the signal to move off east. (A count reveals at least thirty-five.) Open balcony cars were by this time kept only for this sort of operation. The third car from the photographer is one of the thirty-seven acquired from Leith Corporation, the last one of which went for scrap in 1936. The score in what was the first match of that year's championship was Scotland 6, Wales 13, and the trams taking the fans back to the city centre were filled with rejoicing Welsh fans, giving vent to their euphoria in song! Before the match the top six feet of the Murrayfield goal posts were painted red – a daring Welsh affront which was remedied prior to the kick-off.

The North Bridge at 12.45 p.m. on an overcast day in 1933. It is often forgotten that the corresponding South Bridge is in fact a series of sixteen arches, of which only that over the Cowgate is still visible. The busy shops on both sides remove any feeling of a 'bridge'. The complete west elevation of North Bridge was constructed at the turn of the nineteenth century with the *Scotsman* office as its termination to the north. (This is described in *Buildings of Edinburgh* as being 'English Baroque of the Belcher Type'.) The *Scotsman* has now moved to new premises at Holyrood, with its former headquarters being reconstructed into another city centre hotel. Patrick Thomson's fondly remembered store with its open atrium and orchestra used to face the *Scotsman* building. In this picture work is in progress on reconstruction of the tram track, and temporary points will lead the car on to the 'wrong' line. To avoid congestion at the post office junction, several services were temporarily diverted to run via St Andrew Square. Inconsiderate parking has meant that the queuing traffic at the High Street traffic lights has been forced to block the tramlines.

At the top of Waverley Steps were loading islands much used by passengers from the station waiting for trams. Two important landmarks on Calton Hill are visible in this 1934 scene – Nelson's Monument (with the massive ball which drops at noon so that mariners in far off Leith could set their chronometers accurately), and 'Edinburgh's Disgrace'. This is the unfinished Parthenon lookalike which was conceived as a memorial to the fallen of the Napoleonic Wars. Started in 1826, work came to a halt after three years when the money raised ran out. None of the subsequent schemes for its completion have ever gone ahead. Tram 337 on service 3 to Stenhouse (an extension opened in July 1930) represents what could be termed Edinburgh's standard tramcar of that time – thoroughly modern but still fundamentally based upon a design of thirty years earlier. Woolworth's cafe on the second floor of their building (left) was a favourite vantage point from which to survey the busy scene.

This unusual Edinburgh horse railway was used to transport stone at the Blackford quarry, which operated for over a hundred years from the 1820s. Just to the west of the quarry in the Braid Burn valley is the noted Agassiz rock. In 1844 the Swiss geologist Louis Agassiz, having observed the striations – or grooves – on the rock's surface, declared 'This is the work of ice', confirming the glaciated nature of the topography of the area. Blackford Hill itself is a volcanic plug – the remains of the core of a two million year old volcano, left in place as the glacier gouged out the Jordan Burn to the north and Braid Burn to the south. The whole area was acquired as public open space by Edinburgh City Council in 1884 at a cost of £8,000. The quarry supplied hard volcanic andesite for road chippings, although its location at the base of the hill surmounted by the Royal Observatory was not considered very practical. Following a Public Enquiry in 1952, when permission was refused to extend the quarry, it closed shortly thereafter.

Edinburgh had many suburban railway stations, plus quite a number in the inner suburbs, although the trains could not compete with the tramways for short trips. This late 1920s view of Abbeyhill Station shows a local service – possibly from North Leith Station via Bonnington and Easter Road – heading for Waverley. Abbeyhill was opened by the North British Railway in 1869 and lasted (surprisingly) until 1964. The brick-built Holyrood Laundry and its chimney, a former local institution which many years ago 'did for' the author's family, can be seen in the background. The diminutive tank engine is one of twenty-four similar examples built at Cowlairs, Glasgow, in 1881. As number 104 this one was originally named *Roslin*, which was a good indication of its usual sphere of operation. It was scrapped *c*.1931.

A stranger in town! No. 11213, a diminutive saddle tank originally built by the Lancashire and Yorkshire Railway, was photographed on 11 October 1930 at the former Caledonian Railway locomotive depot at Dalry Road. Both the Caledonian and North British Railways had need for such locomotives to shunt round the tight curves of the many private sidings and docks in the city and Leith. Note the highly (un)sophisticated spark arrester arrangement. The barrels in the foreground probably contained lubricating grease. Dalry Road was the Caledonian's main locomotive depot for the Edinburgh area, occupying the triangular area between the diverging lines to Leith and Carstairs. It was completely removed after closure in 1965 and the whole track bed is now incorporated within Edinburgh's Western Approach Road, which does however make good use of bridges constructed over 100 years earlier to serve railway needs.

Prior to the days of the National Health Service, funds to support Edinburgh Royal Infirmary came largely from bequests, donations, company contributions, and the annual parade or pageant of decorated floats. The Corporation Transport Department gave unstinted support to this event every year. This is their AEC breakdown lorry No. 4, one of only a few vehicles actually built for the purpose (most being 'recycled' old buses). The scale model cable tram on this float, bearing the legend 'A Relic of the Past', was taken out of store each year for the event. It is believed that it was made for use as an exhibit in a court case but details have yet to be tracked down. The lorry is decorated with patriotic red, white and blue bunting, shields, and a picture of King George V. The photograph was taken in Holyrood Park, from the slope below James Clerk's School.

Another year, another pageant (did it rain every year?). These three-wheeled 'tructractors' – as they were known before the term dumper truck came into use – built by the Millar's Machinery Company were more often to be found carrying concrete for the foundations of tramway extensions. The scene is again Holyrood Park, this time looking north from the Queen's Drive to one of Holyrood's less memorable features – the gasworks. (Who decided that the most appropriate neighbours for the royal residence at Holyrood Palace were major breweries and a gasworks?) These have all now gone – the former to be replaced, eventually, by the new Scottish Parliament building, the latter by an exceedingly popular attraction, 'Our Dynamic Earth', telling the story of the Earth's development. Without the hype, and at a cost of £34 million (one-twentieth of the price of the Millennium Dome), it has already established itself as one of Edinburgh's prime attractions.

The view over Duddingston village to the fertile fields of East Lothian and the sea was what those taking the Corporation's Queen's Drive tour around Arthur's Seat could expect to see on a good day. (Despite the park then being the King's Park, this was always the *Queen's* Drive.) Edinburgh's former volcano was protected as open space from the mid-sixteenth century, but the carriage drive was a Victorian addition. The park contains (well concealed) remains of four prehistoric forts, plus cultivation terraces of medieval or earlier date. Bonnie Prince Charlie lodged in the village of Duddingston prior to the battle of Prestonpans in 1745, and the adjacent Duddingston Loch is now a bird and wildfowl sanctuary. For their tour on this sunny day in 1930, these tourists have chosen the Corporation's Morris Commercial Viceroy coach SC7282, with its dove grey and deep red livery.

A panorama of Holyrood Palace and the old parade ground, here being used as a car park for the Royal Garden Party during the General Assembly of the Church of Scotland. Frequently also accompanied by inclement weather, on this 1930s occasion it was the number of cars which occasioned comment – over 1,500. The viewpoint is precisely that adopted by the thousands of spectators who watched the grand Volunteer Reviews of Victoria's reign. The first of these, the Royal Scottish Volunteer Review, took place before the Queen on 7 August 1860, with more than 22,000 troops and five times as many spectators. Another was held on 25 August 1881 but unfortunately the heavens opened and the event was ever after known as the 'Wet Review'. No fewer than 40,000 Volunteers were on parade – the largest congregation of men-at-arms in Scotland since James IV marched disastrously to Flodden Field.

In February 1934 A. M. Carmichael, Public Works Contractors, whose head office was then in George Street, purchased this four ton lorry from Albion Motors of Glasgow. A special feature was its three-way hydraulic tipping mechanism. In the thirties Carmichael's plant yard was at West Craigs Quarry, Corstorphine. The company undertook many major civil engineering contracts throughout Scotland, including building dams for the Galloway Water Power Company, and much of the original A8 Edinburgh to Glasgow main road between 1924 and 1934. One of their contracts was for construction of a new road to link the Maybury Roadhouse with the Barnton Hotel (Maybury Road) – opened in April 1927. This was part of a foresighted scheme to improve communications to Leith and included – also built by Carmichael – Telford Road which was opened in 1929. The company was heavily involved in the hydroelectric schemes of the 1950s.

Wm. Dobson had a haulage contracting firm based at Yeaman Lane off Dundee Street, Fountainbridge. This 4½-ton end tipper, (BSG539) with body built by Jackson of Dunfermline, was supplied in April 1938. The tipping gear was hand operated on the racks seen below the raised body. When the racks were lowered they must have been vulnerable to damage from below, and it is perhaps not surprising that hydraulics eventually prevailed. Dobson's lorries, with their dark green paintwork, always seemed particularly well turned out for 'workhorse' vehicles.

The Lord Provost of Edinburgh's official vehicle in the early 1930s was this fine 35 or 45 hp Daimler, seen in Regent Terrace with its smartly liveried chauffeur. The car of the senior elected official is always registered S0 as the city was apparently too slow to acquire S1 when numbers were first issued in 1903. Special arrangements had to be made to allow issue of S0, as the owner of S1 (Lord Chief Justice Sir Norman Macdonald) would not relinquish it. Glasgow followed suit; their first lord provost's car was G4, but they also obtained permission to issue G0. Both S0 and G0 are still in use for the official cars of the leaders of the respective councils. On the right are the railings of London Road Gardens, while behind in the distance Blenheim Place forms a dramatic commencement to London Road itself.

Corporation official cars were maintained and kept at the Central bus garage in Annandale Street. Here two of them are seen outside the parcel office, decorated for the visit of King George V and Queen Mary in 1934 – the note 'as viewed by the King' is written on the back of the print. Central Garage was originally the Edinburgh Exhibition Association hall, built in 1922 when it was considered that the Waverley Market was no longer suitable for their purposes. In 1926 it was purchased by the Corporation for use as a bus garage. While there were large areas of open floor inside, the entrances were not designed for vehicular use, so had to be completely reconstructed. Initially only single deck vehicles could gain entrance.

Continuing a long tradition, the Corporation ran an illuminated tram at the RAF, Aircraft and National Services exhibition, held in Waverley Market in February and March 1939. At the end of its passenger-carrying life, car 221 was given a coat of aluminium-coloured paint and festooned with 500 electric lamps. After touring the system each evening during the exhibition, it was repainted to promote National Service, then by June was carrying slogans for Safety Week. Following a spell in storage, it reappeared in the summer of 1940, devoid of its lighting but painted gold all over for National Savings Week. This 1939 picture was taken at the south side of St Andrew Square. The inner sides of the square were used for SMT service departures (one of their open staired double deck buses is waiting in the background). Further across the square a Corporation bus with an unusual 'streamline' paint style can be discerned.

Work on tram tracks such as this could only be undertaken on Sunday mornings when traffic was minimal – at worst the normal service here meant a car every five minutes. With power (at 550 volts DC) being collected from the overhead wire, the machine in the foreground has one wheel on the track to complete the return electrical circuit. The other wheel is connected to a carborundum block which is being worked back and forth along the rail to grind down any unevenness. Some lengths of rail developed a pattern, or so-called corrugation, which led to very noisy operation when the steel wheel of the tramcar ran over them. The phenomenon was difficult to eradicate, and once in evidence the corrugation spread, requiring speedy attention. Tar boilers, such as the one in the background, were an essential piece of road repair equipment. Whin setts were normally jointed with run-in molten tar or bitumen supplied in large lumps and melted in such a boiler.

Edinburgh's suburban railways could not compete with the rise of commuter car ownership. The line via Davidson's Mains to Barnton (originally known as Cramond Bridge) was a late addition, opening on 1 March 1894. The name change came in 1903. The terminus at Barnton was, at that time, in open fields, but development quickly followed and for many years the station was very busy. Most of the residents who occupied the new housing quickly aspired to car ownership, however, and use of the line and its intermediate stations declined. This is the last train of all seen leaving the small terminus on its final run to Princes Street Station on 5 May 1951. The locomotive is fifty-year-old former Caledonian Railway 0-4-4 tank engine No. 55229 which spent many years working on the Edinburgh branch lines. The station buildings have been replaced by small shops whose users are now frequently deafened by the commuter jet planes on the flight path of Edinburgh Airport.

Locomotives of the former Caledonian Railway were still much in evidence when the last train for Peebles (seen here) left the former Caledonian terminus at Edinburgh's Princes Street Station on 5 February 1962. The station was closed to all traffic three years later on 6 September 1965. This was the Caledonian's second Edinburgh terminus, the first was an unpretentious building in what later became the goods yard to the south of this structure. To call its successor 'Princes Street' was stretching precision, as it, too, was technically still in Lothian Road, but no doubt the label sounded more appropriate for this, their grand new Edinburgh terminus. The site of the railway and goods yard has been taken over by uninspiring cluttered development around Festival Square.

The former North British Railway built its first workshops at St Margarets in the Willowbrae area. The original locomotive shed was this roundhouse with sixteen tracks off the central turntable. Although it lost its roof in a 1930s fire, and its walls soon after, it remained in use until April 1967. In this June 1956 view former North British locomotives are still much in evidence. After demolition of the main building, on the opposite side of the main line, the author was surprised to see while travelling by train from Longniddry to Haymarket, standing alone and resplendent among the dereliction the preserved *Sir Nigel Gresley*. Following its demolition, this part of the site was used to form Edinburgh's 1970 Commonwealth Games stadium.

An important Edinburgh junction, now only a memory: the foot of Leith Street looking down Broughton Street with the disappeared facade of Union Place on the right. The block on the left has also gone, its site now part of the extended John Lewis store. The whole area was blitzed to become a major interchange as part of the misguided Buchanan inner ring road proposals. The roundabout that now occupies this spot once hosted Edinburgh's 'kinetic sculpture', but is now more sedately home to a statue of Sherlock Holmes, whose creator was born on 22 May 1859 at 11 Picardy Place. The Central Fish Restaurant always seemed busy, but especially so at weekends, as was Fairley's Bar and Dance Hall – Leith Street was a 'lively' place of a Friday night. In this photograph one of the ubiquitous PD2s purchased for tram replacement can be seen operating route 8, converted on 3 April 1955. Tram 253 is still operating route 9, which was converted to bus operation on 23 October the same year.

By 1956 the Edinburgh tram fleet consisted almost entirely of these 1934 design Shrubhill built standard cars. (The exception was the unique 180, which many people thought had been retained for preservation, although this was not so). Car 88 takes off down Lothian Road towards Princes Street from the 'Usher Hall' island. The driver is apparently 'watching the Messerschmit bubble car in his mirror. Scooters and bubble cars were a fifties phenomenon, the latter not enjoying the longer lasting appeal of the scooter. This area, which now disgorges the Western Approach Road traffic into a road system designed for the horse and cart, has changed remarkably since it was photographed in 1956. New financial monuments, crammed cheek by jowl into the limited space available without any discernible architectural harmony, appear – to this eye at least – to be the total antithesis of planning and order which went to create much of what Edinburgh is most architecturally admired for today.

York Place – or more accurately here, Picardy Place – was used by a number of tram services heading for Princes Street. This route enabled them to bypass, by going via St Andrew Square, the highly congested junction at the foot of the North Bridge. At one time routes 2, 4, 15, 16, 25 and 26 all served York Place. Three 1934 type Shrubhill trams, 227, 226, and 41, are at the Broughton Street junction, where there was a right-angled crossing used by routes 8 and 9 from Broughton Street (on the left). Substantial reconstruction of Picardy Place has taken place over recent years, with the results not always to everybody's satisfaction. The name Picardy comes from an old weavers village that was once situated nearby, occupied in the early eighteenth century by silk weavers who settled here after being exiled from France. This was also the place where Edinburgh's first traffic lights were installed on 21 March 1928.

For many years brewing was one of Edinburgh's major industries, capitalising on the city's plentiful supply of good clear water. Away from the Canongate, several businesses developed in the Craigmillar area; this busy scene dates from the late 1950s. Bedford NSC816 was a type of vehicle very much favoured by the War Department, and many saw further use in Civvy Street. The William Murray brewery produced 'Wee Murray' light ale and 'Wee Samson' dark heavy. The business was acquired in 1960 by Northern Breweries, part of United Breweries, as part of a major takeover of smaller Scottish brewers. There was infinitely less choice thereafter, with the loss of Jeffrey of Edinburgh, George Younger of Alloa, James Aitken of Falkirk and many others. The Craigmillar brewery eventually closed in 1987.

Ale delivery in the old manner – wooden barrels dropped from the lorry onto a padded sack, then rolled by the drayman to the nearby open trapdoor of the public house cellar where a rope was wound round the barrel to let it down gently on two steep wooden rails. John Aitchison & Company's brewery (founded in 1850) was one of several in the Canongate area. The firm lasted until 1959, when it was absorbed into Hammond's United Breweries. The lorry LFS849 is an Albion 'Clydesdale' supplied in 1953, although the '1/54' on the headstock may imply that 'Aitchie' did not put it into use until the following year.

The archetypal view of Princes Street, with buses and trams both making good use of the width of the street in this 1953 photograph. It shows at least eight buses and ten trams, whilst today a constant procession of buses clog the 'finest street in Europe' from end to end. Capital investment (other than in vehicles) has been all but eliminated, contribution to the rates through profits is a thing of the past, and maintenance of large areas of carriageway at no cost to other users is also now just a memory. No physical evidence is yet to be found of the guided bus-way proposed to run from Edinburgh Airport to the city centre, and opposition from the city's leaders has negated a proposal for a privately funded New Edinburgh Tramway. Even in the USA the wheel has turned full circle, with brand new street electric light rail services constructed in Portland, San Diego and Salt Lake City.

Buses finally replaced the trams in Princes Street in 1956, and in this view the central tram poles are still in place. Such was the outcry in the early 1920s about the effect of such an intrusion into Princes Street that a design competition was held prior to their introduction in 1922. Two of the mass-produced Leyland PD2s – of which Edinburgh purchased several hundred – are operating tram replacement routes 15 and 26. These buses are remembered for their dainty little 'castle' badges on the radiator and by their insubstantiality when compared to the trams they replaced. One commentator described them as 'monstrous masses of shivering tin'. Parking the old Austin here has, in typical fashion, forced the bus out into the other traffic. Note the green litter bin with its very 'Edinburgh' exhortation – 'The amenity of our streets is recommended to your care'!